HOPE WHEN IT HURTS

Where Chronic Pain and Faith Collide

Foreword by

DR. JAMES DICKEY

Book Compiled and Edited by

BEEDA L. SPEIS

DEAR GOD LTD

For permission requests, write to the publisher at:
Dear God Ltd
P.O. Box 451
Vandalia, OH 45377

Previously published as *Letters from the Fold: Seeing God in a Season of Pain*, Copyright © 2024 Beeda L. Speis.

This book is a work of original content and includes Bible verses from various translations. Scripture quotations marked (ESV) are from the ESV Bible (The Holy Bible, English Standard Version ®, copyright © 2001 by Crossway, a publishing ministry of Good News Publishers, Used by permission. All rights reserved.

Scripture quotations marked (NKJV) are from The Holy Bible, New Kings James Version, Copyright © 1979, 1980, 1982 by Thomas Nelson, Inc. Used by permission. All rights reserved.

Scripture quotations marked (NIV) are from The Holy Bible, New International Version ®, NIV®, Copyright © 1973, 1978, 1984, 2011 by Biblica, Inc. ® Used by permission. All rights reserved.

E-Book ASIN : B0DT7SY49T
Paperback ISBN: 979-8-9896966-6-6

Cover design by Dynsof

What People Are Saying

Reading this book was like having a conversation with the Lord, as He lovingly explains - through others - that no matter what we are dealing with, He will be with us to hold our hand as we walk through the situation together.

Pain is not pretty. But it helps to know that God never leaves us alone to work our way through it, and other devastating situations that we might encounter. This is a must read for anyone dealing with pain, be it physical, mental, or spiritual.

Bea L. Hines ~ Journalist at Miami Herald

Hope When It Hurts reminds us that we are not alone in dealing with pain, and that the Lord is the One constant in our healing. As someone who has an autoimmune Disease it is encouraging to be reminded of this.

Pastor Tim Cain ~ Crestview Baptist Church

Hope driven messages bottled up and sent out to the world - where understanding of chronic pain is much needed. I'm glad it made its way to me!

Abbey M. Blue ~ Author of inJustice

I enjoyed reading these well-written personal stories, which encourage readers to draw closer to God and rely on Him for all we need. Each author offers positive ways to accept and rise above circumstances and deepen our relationship with God.

Tracie Heskett ~ Multi-published Author and Blogger

I was blessed to review a proof copy and am firmly convinced it's desperately needed in church libraries and medical waiting rooms. This little book tells the personal tales of those who didn't die from their diseases but learned to live with them. It's both a gut-wrenching and heart-warming read. Our lives carry God's hand-crafted stamp of approval no matter how we look or feel.

Bonnie Evans ~ Author and Contributor

Dedication

This is for everyone suffering from chronic pain. Our families and friends cannot fully understand us. Our physicians won't give us pain medication, so our only option is to suffer through the bad days and do what we can on our good ones.

However, we have access to The Great Physician. He hears our cries. He knows our pain. We may never know the reason for our suffering, but we can have a peace in knowing that everything happens for a reason (Romans 8:28).

Nothing is impossible for our God.

Acknowledgments

Thank you to everyone who contributed to this book. I pray that the stories enclosed are uplifting, inspiring, and encouraging to those who read it. God uses our trials and tribulations for His purposes.

About This Book

What follows are stories from a variety of people. Some are writers, and some are not. Some have long stories to share, and others summarize it in one paragraph. Some were transcribed from an interview, others are in essay format, and still others are organized in an outline. I didn't want to take away from what God called them to share, so there's little editing and a lot of individuality that went into the making of this book.

Please know that any medications, supplements, herbs, exercises, or diets, etc. mentioned in this book are particular to the individual. We're in no way endorsing any solutions or practices as a means of healing from chronic pain. Always consult your doctor before trying anything new.

Foreword

In a world often characterized by busyness and noise, we can easily overlook the quiet struggles endured by those battling chronic pain. Behind closed doors and hidden smiles, lie stories of resilience, courage, and unwavering faith in the face of relentless suffering. It is into this very personal space of vulnerability and perseverance that this book gently invites us. Beeda Speis, along with those who share the challenge of chronic disease, have opened their hearts in *Hope When it Hurts: Where Chronic Pain and Faith Collide* and shared their stories so you might find hope in *your* circumstance.

As I reflect on the pages ahead, I am reminded of the words penned by the Apostle Paul in 2 Corinthians 12:9: *"But he said to me, 'My grace is sufficient for you, for my power is made perfect in weakness.'"* These words echo throughout the testimonies shared within these chapters, as individuals courageously navigate the complexities of chronic pain with a profound trust in the sufficiency of God's grace.

Chronic pain is not merely a physical affliction; it is a multifaceted challenge that encompasses the emotional, spiritual, and relational dimensions of our lives. It disrupts our routines. And the struggle often leaves us grappling with questions of purpose and meaning. But in the midst of all we might face, there is hope—a hope rooted not in the absence of pain but in the abiding presence of a loving and compassionate God.

As you navigate through the stories in Beeda's anthology, you will encounter stories of triumph, and moments of profound vulnerability. In the midst of all that, those struggling remind us how God is helping them work through their continuing challenges. You will hear from individuals who have walked the lonely road of chronic pain and emerged with a deeper understanding of God's faithfulness and a renewed sense of purpose.

But this book is more than just a collection of personal narratives; it is a roadmap for those navigating their own journey through pain. Within these pages, you'll find practical insights as well as spiritual reflections. Above all, *Hope When it Hurts* is a testament to the transformative power of faith—the unshakable belief that even in our darkest moments, we are held secure in the loving embrace of our Heavenly Father.

Beeda's work serves as a reminder that our pain does not define us, but rather serves as a canvas upon which God's grace and mercy can paint a future we never anticipated. As you embark on your own journey through chronic pain, whether as the suffering or the supporter, may you find solace in the knowledge that you are not alone. May you discover the strength and courage to persevere, and the faith to believe that brighter days lie ahead. Thank you, Beeda, for helping to point the way.

With every page turned, may you draw closer to the One who holds your pain *and* your hope in the palm of His hand.

Dr. James Dickey

******

Dr. James Dickey has spent decades communicating the truth of the Bible to congregations, small groups, and online through his teaching blog, *Jacob's Walk*. Jim's efforts continue to be focused on motivating and mobilizing followers of Jesus to finish strong in their efforts for the Kingdom of God. His views are shaped by his family, his career as both a pastor and medical professional, and his love for the truth of Scripture.

His Amazon Author Page:
https://www.amazon.com/stores/author/B07VXQWSGX

Table of Contents

The God Factor

By b. evans

1. I live with two chronic illnesses:

   a. I was diagnosed with arthritis when I was in my early 40's. The medication I tolerate has been increased over the years until I'm now at full dosage (I'm in my 70's). In other words, medically, this is as good as it gets. I do have a prescription for an opiate—I take a half-dose when necessary.

   At this point, many of my joints are swollen and slightly disfigured. My primary issue is that it's now in my spine. Walking, standing, and even sitting can be extremely fatiguing and painful. However, I'm still upright, breathing, and moving.

   b. I was diagnosed with Myasthenia Gravis (MG) when I was 45. It's an autoimmune disease that disrupts the communication between nerves and muscles; it leads to serious muscle weakness. You don't die from it, you learn to live with it. The disease itself doesn't cause pain; but, because muscles are unpredictably weak, it stresses and aggravates every part of the body.

   With the removal of my thymus gland and medication, I do have many 'good' days (70-80% remission). As with all autoimmune diseases, 'good' days are unpredictable. I can't lay low for three days with the promise that the fourth day will be filled with strength.

   For both the arthritis and MG, I have a wonderful walker that allows me to stand and walk upright. It also has a comfortable seat. If my husband holds my

1

hand, I don't need to use it. If I'm alone and have more than a ½ block to travel, I use the walker.

2. How I adapt and persevere:

   a. I pray carefully over my schedule and rely on the Holy Spirit to close and open the doors I'm meant to walk through. I'm still eager to sign up for every good thing that comes along! I can't do that and I know it.

   I don't like to be 'flakey' or let people down, so I'm very cautious about offering tangible assistance to someone else's project. I'm fortunate to have a Christian husband; I usually run everything through his prayers. He cautions me when he thinks I'm doing too much or doing things I don't need to be doing.

   The phrase I have tattooed on my heart is: There's only so much energy for this day, spend it on The Father's Business.

   b. With that strategy in place, I learned to say 'no' to people. When I was younger, people wouldn't believe I had limitations because I 'looked' normal. They tried to manipulate, shame, cajole, and extort help I didn't have to give. I struggled for years to let their words roll off my shoulders; I knew if I didn't hold steady, I wouldn't be able to do the things God called **me** to do. The disapproval and judgments of people I loved and respected added to my distress. ... Since I'm now old (smile), I'm not asked to help with physical tasks as much nor are people as disappointed when I decline.

   c. I also learned to be cautious about requesting prayer at church or Bible studies. I've run into too many well-meaning people who use prayer requests to give advice, compare your troubles with others, or tell you 'if you had enough faith, you wouldn't be sick'.

My husband prays for me every morning and I ask for extra prayers when I'm having a bad day. I have a few close friends I trust with prayer requests but I make them very specific: Prayers for strength to finish something scheduled for that day, prayers for an upcoming doctor's visit, etc.. We believe God can heal me completely of all that ails me; so far, He hasn't said 'yes' or 'no' to those requests. I live every day with a spirit of expectancy but also faith in His Plan for my life. He will accomplish all that He's set out to do in me and through me, whether I'm physically healed or not!

d. I have always been a plan-ahead-person but my illnesses have driven those tactics to new levels. As soon as God asks me to do something, I lay it out on paper with a timeline. I break it down into small steps I can take every day. This fall, I used an Excel worksheet to lay out a huge project God assured me I could do. It was the scariest mission I've said 'yes' to in years; it got done two days before it was due! Procrastination is not a luxury I can indulge in. I'm simply amazed at how much I'm able to accomplish by focusing on the things God is assigning to **me** and then mapping it out in doable snippets!

e. I'd love to be able to delegate physical tasks to others but the majority of my divine assignments are solo efforts. My husband is very healthy and strong. He can't help with the actual assignment but is always quick to drive me, drop me off at the entrance, help me carry in my 'rolling office', set up tables and chairs, ... and then do it all in reverse when I'm ready to go home. I'm blessed to have a husband who believes God wants to use me in impossible ways. I don't take his encouragement for granted.

3. And then there's the God-factor! I don't know how people live through sorrows and heartaches without God! His constant, quiet goodness is simply astonishing. All of the illnesses I live with have taught me more about Him, His kingdom, and His principles than any sermon or Bible study I've heard. Though I would have never signed up for any of my afflictions!!!—God has used every single one of them to develop the fruit of the Spirit in me, elevate my faith, and teach me scriptural principles from the inside out (experience to understanding).

a. Early in my Christian walk, God showed me I have the gift of Exhortation or Encouragement. My life scripture is 2 Cor 1:3-4, "Blessed be the God and Father of our Lord Jesus Christ, the Father of mercies and God of all comfort, who comforts us in all our tribulation, that we may be able to comfort those who are in any trouble, with the comfort with which we ourselves are comforted by God." NKJV

My afflictions have opened my eyes/ears to see/hear heartaches no one else notices. Sometimes:
- All I can do is add people to my prayer list and pray faithfully
- I can intervene with tangible words or actions of encouragement
- I'm able to help people devise (teach) strategies to cope with their physical limitations

b. Another scripture I return to again and again is 2 Cor 12:9, "My grace is sufficient for you for My strength is made perfect in weakness." Whether from arthritis or MG, *weakness* is one of my greatest enemies. This verse holds many levels of meaning for me. When He sends me to do something I know I'm physically not able to do, faith assures me He'll show up just when it's needed and accomplish exactly what needs to be done. And, then He gets ALL the glory! He shines brighter because I'm weak.

c. I purposed in my heart and mind years ago to NOT choose bitterness. Yes, it does sneak in occasionally and tries to turn my heart toward despair and/or hopelessness. It's the verse in Hebrews 12:15 that keeps me from surrendering ... it would not only affect my well-being, but it would 'spring up and defile many.' Exactly the opposite effect I want my life to have.

d. Though he may or may not have been a Christian when he said this, I heard Doctor Stephen Hawking (ALS) say, "There aren't enough hours in the day to do all the things I CAN do, why should I be disappointed in all the things I can't do."

When he made that statement, he was crumpled up in an automated wheelchair and could only move one little muscle under his left eye. He prepared the speech and stored it on his computer ahead of time. During the lecture, he'd twitch his one working muscle to cue each sentence. It was a profound, life-changing moment for me. I'd been overwhelmed with grief over all my MG losses—all I could see was what I'd lost. Doctor Hawking took my focus from what I couldn't do to what I *could do*! And then, he inspired me to think outside the box on how to use what I was able to do!

e. In Closing ... I've taken classes from my insurance carrier and gleaned quite a few helpful coping tools. But, I credit the Holy Spirit with most of the creative life-skill-adaptations I use! That stated, the only other general advice I offer and urge is to have consistent, personal fellowship with God.

When we first got saved and Spirit-filled in 1975, quiet time was a common topic and theme. Back then, my children were babies so I'd snatch time wherever and whenever the moment arrived. I grew in Him despite my sporadic schedule and snippets of fellowship.

My quiet time now is significantly different. Years ago, He called me to get up at zero-dark-thirty for time with Him. Those early morning hours of fellowship are an incalculable treasure. It's transformed me and our relationship. When the house is dark and silent, I'm more sensitive to His Spirit and what He's speaking. It's so much easier to see what He wants ME to do and where I've gotten off track. It's also when He pours a unique creativity into me and then shows me how and where to pour it out.

Though I have listed it last, it's actually the most powerful piece of advice I could offer to anyone. If you're living with physical (or mental, emotional needs), set aside a specific time of the day to spend in His presence. Sing, pray, listen, read His Word. Spending time with the One who knit me together in my mother's womb ... who knows me better than I know myself ... who sees the 'full' picture of who I am and why I'm here – priceless!

"Oh Lord, You have hidden me in the secret place of your presence." Psalm 31:20

****

b.evans shared a note with me that I would like to share with you. She wrote:

Beeda, I'm aware I have resources other people may not have (a supportive mate, health insurance, we're not rich but we have financial security) ... However, I'm convinced beyond a shadow of a doubt God will give every single person who is asked to walk the path of afflictions the very support they need to endure to the end. My prayer is [this book] and others like [it] will inspire them to look for the 'way of escape' God has provided.

Thank you for your work and research for those who suffer. I hope we get to meet someday. Til then, His servant and your compadre in The Father's Business. B.E.

****

About the Author:

b. evans lives in a rural county in Northern California.

In addition to the healing and sustaining power of God in my life, I am fortunate to have a supportive Christian husband and good health insurance.

Rescued

By Carmen Leal

On June 18, 2015 we were at a red light after a perfect day at the beach. We were driving a small Subaru and a large SUV slammed into us going about 20 MPH. We hit a second SUV and three other cars for a five-car pileup.

The car was totaled and I thought I was unhurt. Nope. I suffered a severe concussion, tore a muscle in my neck and another in my back. My head either hit my cell phone or my cell phone hit my head, I don't remember, but it resulted in blunt force trauma and a traumatic brain injury. I was a passenger texting to get an address for book club.

In the beginning my doctor tried to treat it all without drugs. HUGE mistake. Acupuncture, massage, manipulation (he was an osteopath,) and more. After four months of sleep deprivation and a level 10 headache every single day, I was suicidal. The wreck left me with visual hallucinations and I never slept. The neurologist mapped my brain and saw that my brain was only 10% awake and so we moved on to drugs. So many drugs that didn't work.

My doctor suggested I get a dog and I said no. Not a dog person. I suffered for 18 months with no noticeable relief and finally decided I could not keep working to support us, I made more than my husband, so we eventually moved from Hawaii to Wisconsin. Talk about wanting to kill myself.

Sadly, alternative healthcare such as massage and reflexology and other things are not covered in this state. Hawaii was much more progressive. So I do without and I know it's not smart, but I can't pretend to afford the things that help. I take supplements and migraine meds and a sleep aid so I can at least get six hours of sleep most days so I can function. The neck and back pain I just deal with because there's nothing I can do. I walk, do water exercises, and try and monitor my screen time.

In March of 2017 we went to a rescue and adopted a dog who saved my life. Literally. During the next four years, I helped the dog rescue before they became a COVID casualty. I redesigned their website, wrote grants, created events, and pretty much became the face of the rescue. I wrote over 6,500 bios and helped every dog find their forever home.

Last year I wrote a book about rescue dogs and I am working on the second one right now. A portion of every book sold is donated to a foster to adoption rescue group to help them rescue more dogs and to create awareness about the need to adopt.

I find that having a purpose has helped me to put less focus on my pain. I also do not go to places that will trigger my noise induced migraines. No concerts, no farmers markets, no sports. No lots of things.

I lost everything when the wreck happened. I lost living where I felt happier than I have ever been, a job I loved, my church, friends, traditions, and more. I don't hate WI, though I despise the dark of winter, but it's not home.

I can no longer go to church because the music is too loud. Churches that might not be loud don't have a community. We've visited at least thirty churches. It's been hard as a senior in a new community to make friends and start over.

I have found God in the gardens we've slaved to create. I still don't like gardening but I do like the results and I do find God there.

I joined a choral group and we sing at least 98% religious works and I find God in the music. I find God in volunteering, in helping people who have it so much worse than I do.

God has used me to help others who are suicidal, who feel like they have no reason to live. I know God is not only in the church. I find him in books, in podcasts, in prayer, in getting up each day even when I don't want to.

My headaches are usually a level 4-5 which is still bad, but at least they are better. It takes time to heal a brain. And I have to accept that I'm not the me I used to be.

****

About the Author:
Carmen Leal is a storyteller and the author of multiple books, articles, devotionals, and human-interest stories. Carmen relocated from Hawaii to Oshkosh, yes, there is a story behind the move, and has become an awesome dog mom. Carmen and her husband have become reluctant gardeners and know a crazy amount about Wisconsin weeds. Carmen's faith, wit, humor, and poignant personal observations, coupled with her down-to-earth style and common-sense approach to dealing with life, make her a popular presenter as she inspires and motivates people of all ages and walks of life. Carmenleal.com

Closer To God

By Nana Deb

I've had RA (Rheumatoid Arthritis) since 2009, and have been on medicine for it ever since. In addition to Methotrexate pills, I get a weekly Orencia shot, and have to see my doctor every three months. She does bloodwork regularly to monitor my liver. It wasn't prescribed, but I've tried to maintain a healthy diet consisting mostly of vegetables, along with supplements and pain creams. Even with all of this, RA has hindered me from doing certain things.

My faith in God has helped me through so much of my RA journey. Because of the excessive pain, I find myself praying more and asking for relief. This keeps my focus on God. I can rest in His care.

There have been many days where the fatigue from RA has been debilitating, and it's during those times, especially, that I lean on "Be still and know that I am God" (Psalm 46:10). God answers my prayers for strength and energy. He has gotten me through many days when I didn't think I could do it.

I rely on God because my pain and fatigue require it. I can't live like this apart from God, and that's a big positive for me.

I went through a really stressful time a few years back and found myself praying even more than usual. The stress caused my RA pain to flare up to an unbearable level. I couldn't even raise my arms. I had no choice but to hand it over to God. He showed me that I had to give up on a close relationship. When I finally did, the pain went away. It was an aha moment, revealing God's presence.

****

About the Author:

Nana Deb lives in Brookville, Ohio with her loving and supportive husband. She has a card ministry which ministers to those going through difficult times, and she writes to persecuted Christians across the globe.

Chosen: My Journey to Radical Acceptance

By Angie Clayton

In the summer of 2019, I thought I had an infection. However, after three rounds of antibiotics, I was sicker than ever and desperate for answers. I saw a specialist, who gave me a diagnosis but wasn't able to solve the problem. By the time I got to a neurologist, I had lost sensation in much of the lower half of my body - he diagnosed me with MS, did a lumbar puncture and sent me for five days of massive steroid infusions. I felt better after the first one, and I truly believe he kept me from paralysis and possibly saved my life.

My lumbar puncture results puzzled him, however, as they did not match up with an MS diagnosis and suggested another problem. He sent me to an MS specialist at a teaching hospital in our city, and that neurologist diagnosed me immediately with a severe episode of transverse myelitis, and neurosarcoidosis. Both were totally unfamiliar, and as I tried to take in all the things he was telling us, all I could really hear was "progressive" and "no cure." He started me on a regimen of drugs, with the goal of keeping me stabilized.

As I look back, I was experiencing symptoms as early as 1990, all of which were treated independently with marginal success and some really lousy experiences with lousy doctors. More than one suggested it was "all in my head" and recommended that I see a psychiatrist. One accused me of faking my symptoms, and another accused me of drug seeking. As the months and years went by, more and more and more health problems emerged, and I was starting to wonder if it WAS all in my head.

Neurosarcoidosis is extremely rare – if affects about two in a million people. It's an autoimmune condition, which basically means that my immune system attacks itself instead of protecting me. I have lesions on my spinal cord and in my brain, deal with migraines and seizures, large and small fiber neuropathy, memory loss, heat and cold intolerance and autoimmune chronic fatigue.

It's a subcategory of sarcoidosis ("sarc"), also rare, which primarily affects the lungs. Although I didn't have symptoms at the time, a CT scan revealed a number of small nodules in my lungs. Right now, those are in the category of "watch and wait," as are several lesions on my liver. "Sarc goes where sarc wants" – this is the song of my tribe. Every part of the body is at risk - eyes, heart, liver, kidneys, spleen, digestive system, joints, muscles. Each could be invaded at any time, some with extreme results, so I must be vigilant with any physical symptoms I experience. They all must be examined through the filter of sarc.

At last count I have 19 doctors.

We named "it" Loco before I was even diagnosed, because what was happening to my body felt both insane and unknowable. My husband has been by my side throughout, and he is very much affected by it – by naming it, it is its own thing, not just me and not just him.

I have flares pretty often, and those are scary because rarely do I recover what is lost. I have quite a lot of pain all the time and have had three hip replacements and three shoulder surgeries, among others. I am exhausted. All of this is worse during a flare, and usually there are some new symptoms as well.

My neurologist is so great, and the hospital is amazing – they do sarc research, and as a result almost all of the doctors I've seen are well versed and up to date with my condition before they see me. Right now, I am stable with meds – steroids, an antimetabolite that is also an old chemo drug, and stimulants to combat the fatigue.

The neuropathy is rough, but fatigue is the most difficult physical symptom I experience right now. It is often debilitating, requiring multiple naps each day. I have had to learn to respect my body and set goals accordingly - if I don't, the result is failure and disappointment and guilt. Do I wish I had more energy? Of course. But the reality is that I don't, and no amount of wishing will change that.

Probably the most detrimental thing that has happened on this journey I have done to myself – it's called Google. I lived in fear of the what-ifs and projected out every new symptom to its worst-case scenario. I was depressed and anxious on top of not feeling well, ever. Becoming aware of this, and choosing to stay away from the Google as well as not letting my imagination run away from me – these things have truly been more beneficial to me than any medical intervention.

There is no "normal" for me anymore, and I've finally stopped trying to find one. Today, this day, is where I must choose to live. Balancing vigilance with staying present in the moment is a challenge, to be sure, but as I've practiced it's gotten easier. This lesson has carried over into the rest of my life, and the difference is incredible. Today isn't always terrific, but worrying about tomorrow won't change a thing and is a big waste of my energy, which is in short supply!

The future is unknowable to me, but I can rest in the hands of the One who does know. I am not defined by neurosarc – I have it, it does not have me.

Here's what I know – I am chosen for this. CHOSEN. Does that sound strange? But if I believe what the following verses say (and I do), then that means my neurosarc was planned for me from before time began. It means that He has plans for me that are good, and He made them knowing the physical limitations I would face.

> You saw me before I was born. Every day of my life was recorded in your book. Every moment was laid out before a single day had passed. How precious are your thoughts about me, O God. They cannot be numbered! (Psalm 139:16-17 NLT)

> "For I know the plans I have for you," says the Lord. "They are plans for good and not for disaster, to give you a future and a hope." (Jeremiah 29:11 NLT)

Can you see how that changed everything for me? If I'm chosen for neurosarc (or anything else that comes my way), that makes it is a privilege. Every choice, every response, every word should reflect this truth: My physical condition is not something I'm simply enduring. Instead, I am embracing it as best I can because people are watching.

No, that doesn't mean I'm going to say "I'm fine" when I'm not. That's lying. But I also refuse to run around moaning and fretting and complaining with an "it's not fair" attitude – my mental and spiritual well-being depend on it.

I've slowly learned surrender, about being still and quiet, and now can rest in this truth:

The Lord will fight for you; you need only to be still. (Exodus 14:14 NIV)

And waiting. Oh how I've learned about waiting! I know how to wait impatiently, anxiously, fretfully ... and I now know how to wait patiently and without fear, no matter how I feel.

Yet those who wait for the Lord will gain new strength. They will mount up with wings like eagles, they will run and not get tired, they will walk and not become weary." (Isaiah 40:31 NASB)

This little poem is on my whiteboard in my office, and I think it will always stay there:

We thought these lives were our own.
It seems we were mistaken.
Bring what is broken
To the hands that first formed it.

When I had to leave my "big" church job in 2014, I was so broken. I felt sidelined and useless, and wondered what is the point of me? I struggled with pain and sickness and surgery after surgery. But one day these verses shouted my name, and they still do:

"But forget all that— it is nothing compared to what I am going to do. For I am about to do something new. See, I have already begun! Do you not see it? I will make a pathway through the wilderness. I will create rivers in the dry wasteland." (Isaiah 43:18-19 NLT)

Had I been able to continue in that job, I would have missed out on so much. What seemed like only wilderness and wasteland at the time has been transformed into something beautiful that never could have happened otherwise. These days I spend a lot of my time with hurting women, and pouring into them is natural and right for me. I also have time to write, which I've wanted to do for as long as I can remember. And I feel like I'm right where I belong.

****

About the Author:

Angie Clayton is an author, speaker, blogger and editor who has a passion for connecting with the hurting. She is a storyteller, and her writing reflects those experiences - her blog, Framing the Days, is rich with diversity. Angie shares the joys and beauty of both the mountaintops and the valleys of her life.

Her book, "Peering into the Tunnel: An Outsider's Look into Grief," is a collection of real stories, as well as helpful suggestions for how to come alongside someone who is grieving.

Angie has been married to Greg for over three decades. They live in the Kansas City area and have two grown children and four grandchildren. Also known as "Nini," Angie loves spending time with them.

Website: angieclayton.net

Email: angie@angieclayton.net

Facebook: Angie Clayton, Author - https://www.facebook.com/framingthedays

Abuse and Survival

By Kathy

Recently, I had a nerve-burning procedure. A couple of family members had it done, and after three to four weeks of intensive pain, one of them never had to have it done again. The other one has it done every six months. I saw an anesthesiologist doctor who specialized in pain. She had needles with heated tips to work on three different areas on the right side of my back. She started cutting nerves with the heated needle. About half an hour later, when I thought we were about done, she goes, "Oh, I'm just plugging you into the machine now to cut the nerves." When I left, it wasn't good. It was pretty painful for at least three or four weeks. I won't be doing that again. It's not worth it to me.

My medical problems started at a young age. At six years old, I had to have bladder and urethra surgery due to the damage caused by my father. He sexually abused me until I became an adult.

My periods were always painful, and I missed a couple of days of school each month because of it. I also had numerous bladder infections.

When I turned eighteen, my mom took me to see her OB-GYN. The doctor realized I had endometriosis and said he could do minor surgery to get rid of the adhesions. The (one) minor surgery turned into several surgeries, leading to my first major one, a reconstructive surgery. The doctor attempted to "rehang" everything that was messed up from endometriosis, like my uterus and all that. After the surgery, the doctor told me that he cut the nerves in my back so that I wouldn't feel pain if I got pregnant. He told me that when in labor, I would just feel pressure. Even though he stripped the nerves, got rid of the adhesions, and put everything back in place, I was still in a lot of pain. The doctor then suggested that I go on birth control and stay on it so that I wouldn't have periods, which would alleviate my monthly pain. My parents refused the birth control because we were Catholic. I had no choice since I was only nineteen and on their medical insurance.

So, I was put on a medication called Danazol. It made me gain some pounds, but other than that, it didn't do a whole lot. The medicine started messing up my vocal cords. They swelled. I could only whisper. Even all these years later, I still have difficulty projecting my voice and speaking up. I was left with a raspy voice. My left vocal cord still doesn't always work, so my voice cracks and sounds terrible. But that's the least of my medical issues.

A year and a half later, when they went in to do the hysterectomy, they found that my uterus was twice the normal size and bright red. My doctor said, "There is no way you could ever have children." He told me that a second disease had gotten into the walls of the uterus, so...I pretty well knew. I'd never be able to have children.

During that time, I had several infections and was on a variety of antibiotics, which were making me physically ill. Then my parents said, "Okay, okay, we'll put her on birth control," but by then, it was too late. It was just too late.

The hysterectomy surgery was just nine months after I got married. I was only twenty-one years old. During those nine months between getting married and having a hysterectomy, my mom took me to faith healers, hoping I wouldn't have to have the surgery. The faith healers mostly did the laying of hands on me. The whole experience with my mom and the faith healers made me confident that the surgery

22

was what God was telling me to do and that something else, something better, would come along. My prayers were answered. My husband and I were blessed when we adopted a baby girl.

After the surgery, I had horrible UTIs followed by back-to-back kidney infections. I had to set an alarm every six hours, even through the night, to take medicine because the infections wouldn't clear up. Then, all of a sudden, it stopped being an infection and ended up being interstitial cystitis. This bladder disease was even more painful than the endometriosis.

About six years later, I needed another surgery. The doctor didn't remove my ovaries during the hysterectomy so that I could save them to use later, but my husband and I didn't have enough money to have that done. Then, it got to the point when my ovaries had to be removed because I was in so much pain. I didn't know if I could continue working. Having my ovaries removed didn't help anything, but it made the endometriosis stop bleeding inside of me.

The pain just seemed to get worse with every surgery. I had the three major abdominal surgeries: the initial reconstruction and then the hysterectomy, and then lastly, the ovaries taken out. Additionally, I've had sinus surgery, strokes, etc.

Eventually, I was able to go on disability. It was impossible to work while dealing with such intense pain. Shortly afterward, my husband and I were able to adopt a baby girl, as I mentioned before. It went smoothly. Things just worked out. Finally, a blessing amid all the suffering, or so I thought.

My husband and I separated when our daughter was five years old, and we divorced four years later. So, I was a single mom with all of these health issues and chronic pain, trying to take care of a small child and myself. Part of my treatment for the bladder disease required me to drive to Columbus once a week. After a while, I just couldn't keep doing that, so I learned how to give myself the treatments at home.

I was prescribed morphine and Percocet for several years. The truly unfortunate thing about it was that people would find out I had chronic pain and would ask me for pain pills. I never knew if people liked me and my young daughter for ourselves or if they were just being nice to us, so I would give them pills. It was hurtful. I never gave anyone any pills, but they just kept asking.

With everything I've gone through, I know I wouldn't be alive today without God. I know that for a fact because I almost committed suicide at one point.

I had already set up the hotel I was going to and how I would do it. My husband had our daughter for the weekend, and I told him I wanted her to stay there an extra day because I had all these plans. I was going to cut my wrists in the bathtub, and I even picked out what clothes to wear.

I was all packed up, ready to go, but as I walked out the door, I thought, "I need to call (my friend) Marsha because she's gonna wonder where I am." Marsha calls often, which is fine because she's got a lot of medical problems, too. We were meant to be friends. Thankfully, I called her, and she convinced me to call the doctor. That's why I didn't commit suicide. I didn't even end up going to the hotel. It was all God. He made me think of Marsha during a time when I was focused on myself. Marsha was crying at me on the phone, pleading with me until I promised to call my doctor. It turned out that my doctor, who was vacationing in Florida at the time, was unable to get me set up with a hospital, so he insisted that I tell my sisters the next day.

Marsha was furious that the doctor didn't put me somewhere safe, but by then, my suicidal thought process was broken. It wasn't foremost on my mind anymore. So, the next day, I called my sisters and asked them to visit me in the next couple of days. My sister Gwen came over the next day to massage my feet and give me a pedicure to cheer me up. Then I had to tell her what I'd almost done. She just cried. No words. Just tears.

Later, Megan came over, and she cried, too. I just felt like such a loser. But I knew God was on my side, and I did the right thing. I look back now; my daughter, Ashley, was seven years old. It was horrible that I was going to do this at a local hotel, and I realized, "You foolish person." So yeah, God did intervene. With God's help, I was able to recover from wanting to commit suicide. Without God, I wouldn't have made it.

I remember, on top of everything else I was going through, I had terrible diarrhea for two years. I had ulcerative colitis and ulcers inside the intestines. The doctors couldn't figure out why I had any of it. My gastro doctor, who was running all these tests, asked me, "So, will you make a pact with me saying that you won't commit suicide, at least not until after we see each other next time?"

I said, "No, I will not make that commitment." He did it every time I went to see him. He was really a Godsend to me, and it was nice of him, but I just couldn't—I didn't want to be controlled by anybody else. I felt like I had been controlled by others for so much of my life, and I was done with it. But I got over it and never got close to attempting suicide again.

At the time, I just didn't feel like anybody was there for me, anyone I could turn to. I felt very distant from Jesus at the time, too. Over the years, I've gotten into the Bible again. I started reading a study Bible and devotionals, from which I've learned so much. I also have a New Translation Bible, which I enjoy reading. Plus, my next-door neighbor is very, very religious. Her Dad was a Minister. So, she and I sometimes discuss the Bible and various religious topics.

I still have a myriad of health issue. One thing I would say about pain is I will take physical pain over mental pain any day of the week because mental pain is so much worse. It never goes away.

Growing up in the same house with my Dad, we were hit, we were kicked, we were pushed, we were shoved. If you sat beside him at the dinner table, he'd smack you up on the back of the head if he didn't like something you said or did, so, of course, nobody ever wanted to sit next to him.

The first time I started smoking was after I saw a man throw a lit cigarette over the deck at my uncle's house, and I thought, "I want that." I went and picked it up and started smoking. I was eight years old. It's just an indication of how sick I really was with depression and everything else and all the stuff that went on. My mom had a hysterectomy, and while she healed, we were sent to stay at my Aunt and Uncle's. They both smoked, so I'd steal their cigarettes and smoke in my bedroom all the time. Nobody ever caught me.

When I got home, my Mom and I were sitting in the dining room, and the doorbell rang, so she went to answer it just outside the dining room. I picked up one of her cigarettes. I lit it up and started smoking. It was really dumb, but I wasn't that smart then. I'd hide behind our French doors, and my mom said, "I see you. Are you smoking?" And I said, "Yes,

Mom," with an attitude like, "Duh. Can't you see me?" And she said, "Well, put it out," so I did. She had this long talk with me, you know, making me promise to never smoke again and all that, but all of us kids started smoking really young.

When I was fourteen, I started cutting myself. By then, I was numb to the world and just wanted to feel something, anything, even if it was pain by my own hand.

It's an example of just how bad things were. Here I was, smoking at eight years old, cutting myself at fourteen to try to deal with all the abuse. It wasn't just sexual abuse, either. My Dad hit us with belts. He'd line us up, and we had to pull our pants down. He would hit across all of us. I was five, maybe six, and my teacher noticed it because my Dad kept hitting my legs with his belt. I don't know what happened, but he suddenly quit hitting us girls. It just suddenly stopped. I know he did it to my younger brothers, though. It was just things like that. Bad stuff was always going on.

There were so many times throughout my young life when I wondered where Jesus was. Why wasn't He saving us from this horrible Dad?! I remember being aware of foster homes, though, and I was afraid if I told anyone what my Dad did to me that they would take all of us kids away and separate us, and we'd have to live with people who weren't our family. As bad as it got, the thoughts of being separated seemed worse. So, I didn't tell anyone who could have helped me.

My oldest brother, James, didn't seem to be affected like the rest of us. He always took Dad's side. Once James told me, he said, "Now don't you ever blame Dad for all your 'not having kids problems.'" He felt I wasn't having kids because I wanted to be a career woman. And I said, "Have you met me? Cause I love kids." There was always all this stuff going on with all of us. My mom said she never knew about any of it. I find that hard to believe. Every therapist I've had has told me that my mom definitely knew; she maybe didn't realize she knew, but she knew.

I feel so much freer now, and I thank God for that. I'm thankful I didn't end up marrying somebody who was abusive to me and hurt me and all of that because I easily could have fallen into that trap. My husband, Chris, was good to me, but he was extremely critical. My skin would break out in a red, blotchy rash, especially all over my face. Chris just hated it when I did that, as if it was something I could control. He didn't realize that the more he berated me, the more I'd break out. It was a physical reaction to a psychological issue that I had to take medication for. I'd have secondary infections all over, also.

Couples just need to be nice to each other, and let's face it, kindness goes a long way.

I never dated after my divorce. I have no interest in it whatsoever. I'm to the point in my life where I'm not only ready to be honest with myself, but I also want to share what happened to me. At some point, I found Jesus and felt Him cry with me, felt Him hurt with me. After that, I didn't feel alone. I felt strengthened. So much so that I was able to help other family members sue my dad for sexual abuse. My Dad told the court that he "didn't remember." He had a lifetime of lies to take to the grave. I'm thankful that my childhood of lies is out in the open. There are no secrets and, therefore, no chains.

Jesus strengthened me and revealed my purpose in all of this. He gave me the strength to help my abused family members. The court case led to the discovery of sixteen additional teens who were abused by Dad. Afterward, even more came forward.

My Dad later told me that because of my role in getting him prosecuted, he wanted to take me out of the will, but my mother wouldn't let him because I was her daughter, too. I ended up being co-executor of his will, along with one of my sisters.

I'm still not able to forgive my father, but Jesus can. I pray that He gives Dad Divine Mercy. That I can pray for. I confidently trust Jesus now. It took me a long time to get to this point. It feels liberating to "trust in the Lord" (Proverbs 3:5a).

"For I know the plans I have for you," declares the Lord, "plans to prosper you and not to harm you, plans to give you hope and a future." Jeremiah 29:11 NIV

****

My Health Journey

By Deb Damone

I think for me, finding myself near death in ICU several times was not only an eye-opener, but a wake-up call!

When I was about 55 years old (I'm now 70,) my health started really going south! However, I had never really been a healthy specimen, to begin with!

Coming from an unstable home life, being malnourished, by a sick mother, then overfed with rich foods, from my father's mother, would contribute to a faulty foundation for my life ahead.

Of course, family genes would weigh in tremendously! And the final straw would be very bad eating habits, as an adult. I was a sugarholic!!! That eventually, coupled with a sedentary lifestyle, would nearly be my demise.

In 2010, I had founded and began running a mental health organization. The stamina demand and mental acuity required to run the organization, teach, and raise what little financial support to keep afloat, was pretty grueling!

Over time, I had noticed that I was struggling to breathe when I rushed to teach classes! I just assumed it was being too overweight, which I was, plus not being in shape!

But by 2012, I would find myself gasping for air, pleading with GOD for every breath! To make a very long story short..... after a few misdiagnoses, 3 years of searching for answers. I would finally find my way to a Park Ave. Doctor in New York! And it would be Dr. Charney, who would correctly diagnose me with Myasthenia Gravis!!

Myasthenia (MG) is an autoimmune disease that falls under the umbrella of Muscular Dystrophy. The muscles do not respond correctly and become overworked easily.

This diagnosis would finally explain why for years when I worked out at the gym I would become so fatigued and unable to function. Everyone told me I was supposed to feel a bit tired, but this was not normal tiredness!! So now, it became apparent that the MG was nagging in the background for years, before it was fullblown!

I was also diagnosed by another Park Ave Doctor. He found through blood work that I had Lupus, another autoimmune disease, which my father's mother died of, at age 52!!

To say my life would never be the same is an understatement. I needed to lose 50 lbs, to start!! Nevertheless, this would turn our lives upside down and yet also create new opportunities for me, both educationally and financially.

It took months to get on the right medication! In the meantime, due to an inability to move my lungs, I had our ambulance on speed dial! I was constantly in the ER..... and ICU!

In my opinion GOD led my journey! For you see, I was at a complete loss!! I had no clue where to begin! So in a brief synopsis of my journey to holistic measures..... this is my sauntering journey!

A brief, 20 min. meeting with a young woman (in the ER, with me) led me to Doctor Charney, the doc responsible for getting the right med for the correctly assessed ailment.

My niece, unwittingly led me to Dr. Ken Moss, who would help me establish the ability to not become so symptomatic from the MG! It was he, who went to a seminar to deal with MG, to learn how to treat me. It was there that he found out that gluten exacerbated MG..... and ALL autoimmune issues!! From that time on I went gluten-free, and the MG episodes were never as severe.

I began to look into other forms of holistic methods. I learned about, and how to make kefir! Kefir helps rebuild the gut!

My childhood friend introduced me to essential oils. And that's when I went chemical-free!!

I learned about the severe effects of GMO's, antibiotic fed poultry and additives! I kept a journal to learn about my reactions to foods! I stopped using refined sugar, white rice and eating lots of empty calories. I never touched another fast food! I learned the many terms for the neuro-toxin MSG.... And stirred clear of it.

In so doing, coupled with moderate walking, I lost the 50 lbs. and learned more about reading labels and how foods triggered both health and illness!!

I also decided to go to school to become a Clinically certified Aromatherapist! I was already a certified life coach..... now I would couple my aromatherapy knowledge with life coaching and create a business helping others!!

As a result of how ill I had fallen, I closed the mental health agency in 2010.

Once again, now, through my new business, in Aromatherapy, GOD would put someone in my life for a brief moment, at a beauty seminar! She and I would discuss our love for the oils! And during the course of conversation, I would learn how her Mom, who also had MG, used a particular oil to deal with the Myasthenia.

In 2018, I decided to wean off the very expensive medication, Mestinon, that had sustained me, for the last 7 yrs. By 2019, I weaned off that medication completely! And depended on an oil to help with the MG!

I often say, I'm the healthiest, sick person I know! With no less than 5 autoimmune illnesses, 2 of which can be deadly, I am grateful to have learned how to navigate the journey.

****

About the Author:
Deb is the wife of Dennis for 52 yrs come June. They have two children, Desiree' and Dave, and two grafted in thru marriage, Bri and Rachel. They have 10 grandchildren, and three great grandchildren.

Over the course of Deb's life, she's written several books, two of which were autobiographical, and she has also done some editing. She's won awards for her poetry and is included in two additions of the World Woman's Book of Who's Who.

She currently writes a blog on FB, entitled the SWORD OF THE LORD.

Deb has taught scripture for 45 years out of her 49 years as a believer; and is currently teaching a ladies bible class out of her home.

Her life verse is Romans 8:28. Yet when the struggles seem insurmountable, she turns to Psalm 91 and the 23rd Psalm.

Limitations as Loving Boundaries

By J. Bea Wilson

I have never liked limitations and have always pushed hard to get past them. About six months after my only daughter was born in 1998, I endured a series of sinus infections. I was a mom who pushed life hard and did not know how to care for herself well. Taking several courses of antibiotics so I could keep working led to a clostridium infection that took months to clear. I've suffered chronic pain and fatigue since.

For almost a decade, I pushed myself hard to be the best mom, wife, worker, friend. I homeschooled my daughter, led her Girl Scout troop, taught Sunday School, and worked as an editor—all while struggling with chronic health limitations. With no diagnosis other than fibromyalgia and no good effects from medications, I had no solutions to a life of pain and fatigue and struggled with suicidal ideation. In 2007, during a Christian music concert, I acknowledged I'd reached the end of my efforts. I finally surrendered them all to God, and my own pushing to control my life lessened significantly.

In 2010, a challenge I took on a whim to learn to bake allergen-free led me to shop regularly at a natural food store. The owner mistook me for someone with celiac disease, and after learning the symptoms—many of which I had, including gluten ataxia—I started eating allergen-free. Within months, allergic reactions and intolerances that had limited me all my life eased or stopped entirely, including frequent asthma episodes, extended migraines, and debilitating digestive issues.

Feeling freed from so many limitations, I volunteered at the health food store and discovered my husband's health improved off dairy while my daughter's health and learning improved off soy and chemical additives. I believe God led me through diet changes to help myself, my family, and others seeking improved quality of life.

But the more I learned about food health, the harder I pushed myself to learn the keys to healthy living. I began an effort to make drastic changes in many areas of my life, so drastic that they posed challenges to valued relationships. After a few years, the store closed, and with it I lost a lot of the support I needed to keep progressing in my understanding of food health. My health improvements plateaued, and I again struggled to find purpose in a life limited by chronic illness.

Beginning in 2019, God led me into the blessing of relationships with other writers and a season of writing from my experience with disability and disappointment. I've written devotionals on hope and suffering, as well as two novels featuring characters with disabilities, none yet formally published. Through many Spirit-led opportunities, God helped me find my passion as a writer and rediscover a calling I'd wanted to respond to since very young.

Soon, though, I again began to push myself hard, spending long hours on writing and developing connections with other writers, gradually to the detriment of my health and nonwriting relationships. Recently, when I sought a "word of the year" for my writing life, God told me to WAIT on him, as spoken at the end of Psalm 27. While I listened to a Christian song, he told me he loves me even if I don't publish my writing, even if I don't accomplish any "big thing" from my perspective and never take on another significant life project. I do not need to push so hard.

I've found God's offer of peace in limiting circumstances difficult to receive, thinking I needed to push myself hard to change limiting situations. I now understand that pushing hard past limits in my own power is not a path to peace, which

God gives us when we listen to him and rely on his strength, not our own. Learning to rely on him is my lifelong pursuit. Each time I've awakened from a season of pushing too hard, the years of pushing have been less in number. I'm growing in understanding and grateful for God's patience with me.

Again and again, increases in health challenges have slowed me down and stopped excessive striving under my own strength. I see this as the Father's provision. I grew up without an earthly father and have struggled to develop a healthy relationship with the Holy Father from my end. I'm choosing to see the limitations I've experienced on my physical health as loving boundaries he allows. They hold me within the embrace of our good Father's will for me in this life, while preparing my mind and heart for eternity.

****

About the Author:
Freelance editor J. Bea Wilson is on a journey to discover personal sustainability alongside her husband of thirty years and their rescue chihuahua. J. Bea writes stories of triumph over disappointment and is passionate about encouraging other storytellers and people with disability.For more from J. Bea, visit jbeawilson.com and jbeawilson.substack.com, and find jbeawilson on Instagram and Facebook.

Giving Hope

By Faith Starkweather Browning

I have dealt with Fibromyalgia most of my life, with POTs creeping in several years before Covid. Everything intensified after I had Covid. I have never resented God for all I have dealt with, I always ask what he wants me to do to serve him with every issue. I love to research the reasons why illness start and what I can do naturally to help heal or make things more tolerable. God always put me with someone who needs to hear what I have learned, and to give them hope that things can get better.

****

Chronic Pain

By Binod Dawadi

I suffer from chronic pain all over my body. I couldn't stand and work, but neither could I sit in one place for a long time and work. My body is slim and thin. So, I am very much weak. While traveling to the far areas, I should take a long breath and I should take rest. I can't find any energy in my body. I need love, care and help all the time. It start in 2023. I have not done any treatment and medical care. I don't know why. I tried to care for myself. I eat a balanced diet. I do some exercise and yoga. At last, I have shown this disease to a doctor; they give me some medicines.

Then I had already given up my hope. And I used to think I can't work now and look after my family. Then I saw an invisible God who sees my pains. God help me in my business and automatically I become a rich man from poor man. I give a lots of thanks to God for improving my illness and helping me in my life. To cure this disease is expensive but we should not worry. God will give this disease to anyone who he wishes and he all look, love and care for us so much. Like as for me. So, be optimistic and be patient. We can win and fulfill our dreams.

****

About the Author:
    Binod Dawadi, the author of *The Power of Words*, holds a master's degree in Major English. He has worked on more than 1000 anthologies, and published in various renowned magazines. His vision is to change society through knowledge, so he wants to provide enlightenment to the people through his writing skills. Binod Dawadi lives in Nepal.

Silent Pain

By Joan Patterson

For the first few years after my diagnosis of multiple sclerosis (MS), my only symptoms were fatigue and reduced feeling in my face and left arm. Then the inevitable happened.

The normal activity after the morning alarm interrupted my sleep was to go to the bathroom and begin getting ready to teach high school business classes. My husband also taught at the same school and our two sons were students.

When I took my first step, I almost fell on my face. My right leg stepped forward, but my left foot decided to take a sabbatical and not cooperate. My leg came forward, but my foot didn't lift. My MS had progressed, and now I had a visible reminder.

Every class that day began with an explanation as to why I was stumbling. The principal and school board knew about my disease, but no one else. Now everyone knew.

That evening, I was in charge of a special event. It was for my business students to learn about how businesses operated. As an example for my students, I dressed in business attire which included high-heeled shoes.

Wearing high-heeled shoes with a dropped foot resulted in my foot dragging, and me holding unto the display tables to keep from falling. Noticing my awkward gait, my husband, Chas, suggested I change shoes into the flat, comfortable ones I wore in the classroom.

[1]"I can't. My school shoes don't go with this outfit. Besides, they're old and scuffed from being dragged all day. Definitely not very professional-looking."

"You don't look very professional anyway holding onto each table like that," Chas told me bluntly. "You have to take those off before you fall and break a bone."

"I'll be okay!" I insisted.

"No, you won't. Go change your shoes."

As much as I didn't want to admit it, I knew my husband was right. I headed for the back room with a fake smile on my face. I wasn't going to allow anyone to see the hurt I was feeling. Entering the room, I snatched up the shoe box in which I'd brought my change of high heels to school. It still held the original tissue paper in which this beautiful pair of shoes had been wrapped for protection from the scratches of life.

Lifting the lid, I took off one shoe and wrapped it in its tissue paper, then gently settled it into the box. *One sign of my femininity laid to rest!*

As I removed my other shoe and wrapped it up, tears dampened the tissue paper. When I reluctantly tucked the shoe into its resting place, it felt as though my womanliness had just died. My very image of myself now lay buried with those beautiful high heels in the casket of a cardboard box. Clutching my treasure to my chest, I silently wept at the death of who I'd been—an attractive, feminine, vivacious woman.

---

[1] . Joan Patterson, *A Matter of Faith; Surviving Life's Crises with Four Wheels, Four Paws, and a Loving God* (Amazon: Joan Patterson Publishing, 2022), 4, 5.

People won't look at me as they did before. They'll see me as a cripple unable to do things for myself and needing pity. I don't want pity![2]

A trip to the doctor confirmed my foot drop was permanent. I now sported a brace to hold it in position. It started on the bottom of my foot and continued up the back of my leg to my knee. Humiliated, I had a choice. Either I could continue holding onto the silent pain of losing my femininity, or accept my condition and continue doing and enjoying what I could. I chose the latter.

A few years later, I had my first major flair-up (exacerbation). My weak body couldn't stand or walk. At that time, my husband was home with a bone infection as a result of falling off our porch roof and landing on an upturned nail. He couldn't help. Taking care of us and the house fell on the shoulders of our youngest son, Luke, a high school junior.

One evening, after Luke came home from basketball practice, he came into the living room and told us he had something important to tell us.

"Mom, Dad. I need to tell you that I quit basketball tonight."

"No. You can't. Your team is in the play-offs. They need you. You're co-captain. Please don't quit now," I said.

"Mom, there are only three things I do, go to school, play basketball, and take care of you and Dad. I can't quit school. I can't quit taking care of you. I can quit basketball."

"I understand, but I don't like it."

With conversation over, he went upstairs to do homework. I sat on the sofa crying. Our son stopped his participation in a sport he excelled at because of my MS. The

---

[2] Patterson, *A Matter of Faith*, 5.

pain of not being able to be a wife and mother overwhelmed me.

My MS progressed which caused me to change methods of how I traveled through each day. My first change was a quad-cane. This was a cane with four feet to stabilize my balance so I didn't examine the floor up close.

Next, came a three-wheeled scooter. My station wagon was fitted with what looked like a little crane to lift my scooter inside. I still walked around the house, but not in public places because distances from one place to another was too far to walk. Using the scooter didn't bother me because many people used scooters. After wearing out two scooters, I progressed to a power chair. Power chairs have two lead-gel batteries to propel them which need charging to keep the chair moving.

After spending many years using my chair, I became adapt at knowing when to plug in the chair to charge the batteries.

[3]One morning, I transferred from my bed to my chair to quickly head toward where most people go when they first awake in the morning. The chair turned on, but instead of a full array of colorful bars, the only ones light were the three red ones and two out of four yellow ones. Not good.

"On no. I forgot to plug in my chair last night, and I have a lot of errands and meetings today. Now what am I going to do?" My stress level rising.

Preparing for my active day, I kept glancing at the battery display hoping somehow more bars would appear by magic. I chided myself for being so forgetful. Negligence would cause me to miss an important meeting unless a

---

[3] Patterson, *A Matter of Faith*, 135.

suitable plan to feed my chair's power supply suddenly happened. One entered my mind and dismissed because everywhere I went people would know right away something was wrong. Explaining my predicament would be too embarrassing. to allow people to see the cost of my forgetfulness. The vision of people scowling at me obviously discussed because of having to be near an electrical outlet gave me shivers. It was the only plan where I wouldn't be confined to the house all day sulking while waiting for my wheelchair to charge.

I spent the day arriving at meetings, locating a suitable electrical outlet, and plugging in the charger and power chair, only to do it all over again. Even worse, the available charge never seemed to increase.

By the time I arrived at my last meeting of the day, both my brain and body were exhausted. At least I'd be in only one room this time. Then it registered that I'd have to move around multiple times. Mainly because this final meeting was the local York White Rose branch of Toastmasters International, which met every other week. Not only would I have to go up front to give the speech I'd prepared for this meeting but also to give my evaluation of other speeches.

So much for getting a good charge! Entering the meeting room, I found an electrical socket, plugged in the charger, then plugged its cord into my wheelchair. Sitting back, I watched the display panel show the power pulsing into the batteries. The power my chair had been craving all day.[4] By the end of the meeting, my personal batteries were in dire need of recharging while my frustration grew with each plug and unplug.

---

[4]Patterson, *A Matter of Faith*, 138.

On my way home, my silent pain from having to adjust my life to mechanical helps began to take its toll. If I didn't have MS, I wouldn't have to have all these extra things. Eventually, I realized what God had been telling me; how blessed I was to have all the means to make my disability more manageable. Not everyone has the resources to help them with their shortcomings.

These examples show times when the silent pain of not being able to live up to my own expectations hit me squarely in the face. My external persona belied my internal confusion. Each time my choice was to either give into it, or accept my condition and move on. With reflection, I usually accepted my condition. Sometimes I made the wrong choice, but God was patient with me, and continued to love me faithfully.

****

About the Author:
Career educator, author, and speaker Joan Patterson received a Bachelor of Science in education and business and an associate degree in Bible from Liberty University. More than three decades of multiple sclerosis (MS) have confined Joan to a wheelchair, from which she communicates passionately the life lessons God has taught her through service dog companions Faith and Giles. Joan has had articles published in various anthologies, magazines, and newspapers. Joan has spoken to churches, women's groups, children's groups, civic groups, schools, nursing homes, and professional groups.

Workaholic

By Bill Behnken

It started back at the end of February, first of March in 2023, but I was just diagnosed about 6 months ago. I went to an RA doctor, had some testing done, and a lot of blood work. I was then told that I had rheumatoid arthritis.

I'm having flare-ups on a regular basis. It goes from my hands to my elbows, my shoulders, hips, and my knee. So right now I'm having a flare up in my right hip, and my right forearm, and it's fairly bad.

I can't even turn my hand or write anything and I just have pain through my arm. It prevents me from doing anything. It shuts me down for a few days. The pain is like a bad muscle pain. Eventually, it goes away and I might feel better for a day or two, until the next time. Wherever it decides to rear its ugly, little head, it'll attack that area. Then I have pain again for one or two days and then start healing the third day, and on the fourth day, I'm back to normal again.

Your normal, you know, you just have to learn what your normal is. There's a lot of feelings that go on with that. It's hard to be cheerful. Then, you make a wrong turn or move a certain direction and it sends an icy, sharp pain through your arm or leg. It's debilitating.

My doctor suggested I start with some medication to help with the symptoms, but I told her that I didn't want to do that without first doing some research. At the time, I was medicine free and so I wanted to find a more natural way to deal with this.

We got involved with Deb Damone (see her story on page 28), using essential oils on a regular basis, but we're always looking for complimentary, holistic medicine. My wife, Sheryl and I did our own research and found a naturalist doctor down in West Chester at the Cole Center. The doctor is doing some tests on me to try to figure out the perfect, natural medicine that will work specifically for me.

Now that a couple of months have gone by, I believe we might be getting closer to a proper test dose to start treating my symptoms that will help me to have less RA attacks, or less duration of attacks. We're getting close to that.

In the meantime, the RA flare ups have made it impossible to work on a regular basis. I'll continue to work outside as long as I can, but right now, it's hard. I came in from working out at the barn at 4 o'clock and my right arm was killing me. I told my wife, I said, I'm done. I'll probably be in the house tomorrow and Friday because of the pain. I also told her, "You might have to wipe my butt cause I don't know if I get back there."

But she told me, "Well, you're on your own. Use your other hand." We had a good laugh. My wife is so wonderful and supportive.

I'm just trying to work through the pain.

This unpredictable pain is one of the reasons why I went ahead and retired early. I couldn't do the physical work that I had done for the last 35 years without losing my sanity. I'm irritable and the pain is just terrible. I thought if I slowed down a little bit, adjusting my work style, I could continue to work somehow, whenever I wasn't having a flare-up.

The big thing, looking back on it, is before I had my flare ups, before I sold my business, I was a workaholic. That's probably part of the reason why I got a divorce on my first marriage. It was a four generation family business. I raised two boys and the business was here at our house. I would work in the field as many hours or more as the guys and that would be fifty to fifty-five hours a week. Then, I still had a couple hours of work each morning, and two, three, four hours of work to do in the evening.

I mean, I was averaging probably six twelve hour days and then some on Sunday. But, when the boys or my wife, my first wife, had stuff to do, I went with them because my office was here in the house, so I could just shut down and take off. However, there were a lot of times when I chose the business over everything else because I had to get quotes or invoices out.

I didn't go to church very much because I was working some on Sundays. I was not honoring God through the last 30 some years of my business.

Once I sold the business, a lot of those duties that I had to do as a business owner went away because they were doing it. However, I still worked all the hours that I could possibly work because Sheryl retired so I was the only bread winner. I thought I need to work as long as I feel good. I need to keep working as much as I can. When I was initially hit with RA, I thought maybe that was God saying, "I don't want you working all this time. I want you to do other things." Now, I'm positive, this is Him. He's putting this foot down. I get it. I need to change, now.

I need to be looking at what He wants me to do. I'm not going to sit here on the couch and watch TV all day because I'm retired, that's just not me.

I pray daily. I ask God that if it's His will, to take some of the pain away. I hate asking it because of the pain that He suffered on the cross. It's like my pain is nothing to what He did, and so I feel bad. Still, I want to reach out to Him. But then I realize it's okay to ask Him, because He wants a relationship with us. He wants us to bring everything to Him. I believe this illness is so that I'll slow down and spend more time with Him. Praying makes me feel good because it's what our Father wants, and I get it. It's up to Him. I could be a lot worse, a lot worse.

Now, could I be better in my walk? Yeah, I could be better, but, I'm working that way. I think a lot of us go through several emotions initially when we're diagnosed with something like this. I'm thankful for where I'm at now.

We see my holistic health doctor once every two weeks and he's doing a study. The doctor puts a drop underneath my tongue. I think it's for LDI (low dose immunotherapy). He's trying to find that right dosage because once he finds that, he said he can make almost all my symptoms go away. So there's hope there.

I'm documenting every bit of my flare ups and then I go back down and report to him and he either ups the dosage or decreases the dosage The insurance doesn't pay for it. Pretty expensive out of my pocket, but I would rather be spending it doing this and trying to make me feel better than blowing it on something stupid. We need to be good stewards of our money.

God has a hand in this and he's wanting me to slow down and change my lifestyle.

My wife started studying a lot on diets. We ended up going with almost a hundred percent no sugar or bread, because she said sugar feeds inflammation and so does all bread because it turns into sugar. So, an added bonus is that I've lost 35 pounds. I was 178 and now I'm down to 142 - 143. Sheryl's on the same diet, because it was hard for one person to be on a diet and the other person not to be. This way, we can be supportive for each other and eat the same kind of food.

I just knew that being on a diet would help me. It really has, but I'm still having my flare ups. I just wanna stay as natural as I can. I was on statin for my cholesterol for 20 some years and Sheryl kept bugging me. "You gotta get off of them, you gotta get off of them." She said they're terrible for you, bad. I was on a low dose so I was only on 20 milligrams but that's because my cholesterol during the summer was fine. I was very, very active. I worked and Just burned a lot of calories. The only time my cholesterol went up was when I was not working, which was winter time.

Last winter I was able to go on a diet and keep my numbers down. Through natural means, I was able to quit taking my cholesterol pills. So I was confident the new diet would work for this new problem. I realized, okay, I can do this, and so we're eating all good stuff.

I do splurge. Maybe when we eat out, I'll splurge a little bit. Because of all this weight I loss, my stomach shrank and I don't eat near the food content that I used to. If I do eat bad stuff, I don't need as much. Right? Sheryl has had to take in all of our clothes. Thank goodness she sews.

I hope what I'm doing helps, but if it doesn't then I'll just have to do something different.

I can do all things through Christ who strengthens me. Philippians 4:13 NKJV

Chronic Pain and Lukewarm Faith

By Heather Hart

After almost a year of severe, chronic migraines, I am happy to announce that I am finally feeling better. I'm not 100% yet, but I have had several pain-free days for the first time in ten months.

I am over-the-moon excited and thankful for the relief.

But as much as I clung to God over the past year, I'm sad to say that my faith still suffered.

For months I was unable to read my Bible (or anything else for that matter), and I am struggling to get back into the groove.

For months I cried out to God in pain, and that pain was my entire world. All I thought about was how much it hurt, and how much that pain affected my life. The ball games I missed. How many times I missed church. I had to cancel the Bible study that I led.

Chronic pain changes your life. Your entire life.

I couldn't take care of my family and depended on my family and church family for so much.

During those days, I saw the blessings. When I wasn't crying out to God, I was praising Him.

Yet, now that there is a light at the end of the tunnel, I find myself with a faith that is far from what it was last year at this time.

I am a lukewarm Christian.

Over the course of the past year, my faith has suffered.

I don't know if there was one thing that caused my drift, so much as the whole.

The lack of a daily quiet time. The lack of fellowship with Christian sisters. The lack of time spent in God's Word.

It all adds up and takes a toll.

I tried listening to an audiobook. I tried memorizing Scripture. Worship music was a constant in my home. But still I have drifted.

My heart longs for a relationship with Jesus. The closeness we had before.

But relationships aren't built overnight. And Jesus isn't a genie in a bottle. I can't simply wish our relationship into existence.

Relationships take work. They take time. And they have their ups and downs.

To be honest, I knew my faith was suffering long before I saw the light at the end of the tunnel.

Back around Christmas when things started getting worse instead of better, I knew my faith was taking a hit.

I would lean hard into Jesus and get a temporary lift in my spirits, but the continued pain kept wearing me down.

I would go through spurts of working hard on my faith. Trying to regain the ground I lost. But nothing seemed to help.

So, I clung to the fact that no matter where I felt I was with Jesus, salvation wasn't a feeling but a fact. I know deep in my heart that Jesus loves me beyond measure, no matter how weak my faith is.

Yet, I long to be on fire for Him. The way I was before. And He gently reminds me to stop looking back and to start looking forward.

It's a new day. My hope is in Christ. I am saved by faith. And faith the size of a mustard seed is enough to move mountains.

Thus, I want to share three steps to rekindle your faith when dealing with chronic pain.

3 Steps To Rekindling Your Faith

1.) Remember that God's Love is Unconditional

This is not the end. God is good and His love endures forever.

The love of God endures through chronic pain, and it endures even when my faith has suffered, because God's love is unconditional.

2.) Pray For God to Set Your Heart on Fire

Matthew 7:7 says, "Ask, and it will be given to you; seek, and you will find; knock, and it will be opened to you. "

When we pray and ask God to give us a heart for Him, He won't disappoint. No, it won't happen overnight, but just like a fire starts with kindling, God will start to rekindle our love for Him if we only ask.

3.) Reach Out to Other Believers

For months, I simply wasn't up to leaving the house when my head hurt, and even if I did, I was in my own world of pain. Connecting with others was hard. The people who were praying for me often frustrated me, but I was ashamed to tell them that. I didn't need prayers for healing as much as I needed prayer for strength... but I never shared that.

If I would have reached out to one or two women and formed a small prayer circle, I truly believe it would have made a world of difference. I had women who supported me online, but I shut out the women of my own community. And even the women who supported me online had to reach out to me to find out what my prayer needs were.

I would get frustrated because even while I was dealing with my chronic migraines, life continued around me. I had other, sometimes more important issues in my life, but because I had shut everyone out, I had no local support system. I truly believe this was a major issue. And I knew it was at the time, yet I still never reached out.

Local women constantly offered to help, but I didn't want to be a burden. I should have known their offers were genuine. They would have gladly came over to pray with me, if I would have just asked.

There Is Always Hope

So, if you are in the middle of dealing with chronic pain. I hope these three steps can help you keep your faith strong, or start to rekindle it if it is weak.

I know they are helping me. My journey isn't over, but the light at the end of the tunnel isn't just about being pain free, it's the light of Christ warming my soul.

But what about you?

Has chronic pain affected your relationship with Jesus?

****

About the Author:

Heather Hart is a best-selling and award-winning author. God has given her a heart for ministering to women of all ages; helping them grow in their walk with Christ. Her goal isn't to tell others how to do more, be better, or achieve perfection, it's to point them to Jesus. You can connect with her online at AuthorHeatherHart.com.

Lost and Found

By Allison Hrip

"For I know the plans I have for you," declares the LORD, "plans to prosper you and not to harm you, plans to give you hope and a future. Then you will call on me and come and pray to me, and I will listen to you. You will seek me and find me when you seek me with all your heart. I will be found by you," declares the LORD, "and will bring you back from captivity ..." Jerimiah 29: 11-14 (NIV)

I am grieving. But it's not in the way you might think; I am not grieving the earthly loss of a loved one—my loss is internal. It lives and breathes in the deepest part of me. I lost myself after my husband suffered an unexpected health event that changed our lives forever. The months that followed stole my identity, or rather revealed my shortcomings. They tested my faith in myself and in God. The woman I'd been up until that point vanished, and I lost my way in the world.

My husband suffered a stroke in 2017, which began a months-long season of multiple TIAs, ambulance rides, ER visits, and a constant reverberating sense of fear that undergirded our family's everyday lives. I remember visiting my primary care physician of over 20 years who treated both me and my husband, and she told me very clearly that I had better take care of myself during this time or it will be my undoing. Although I took her seriously, I did not heed her warning, mostly because it was vague. I didn't know exactly what she meant or what to do about it. Her words foreshadowed my pain.

I praise God that my husband is doing well with little to no lingering effects. However, the emotional, psychological, and spiritual effects linger ... and in ways you might not expect. For me, this season revealed aspects of my being that I neglected over the years—issues of self I had let go of in favor of caring for others, like creating positive habits and establishing healthy boundaries. Clearly, something had to give and neglecting my needs was bound to catch up with me.

I was diagnosed with Fibromyalgia (from two different rheumatologists) about a year after these events. I began to have widespread, unrelenting pain and was first diagnosed with Lyme disease, but the treatment did nothing. My nurse practitioner referred me to a rheumatologist for further testing. All I knew was that I felt like my body betrayed me. I lost all trust in myself. I was unable to live life with any sense of what I *could* or *couldn't* do. I was afraid to travel, work, even attend social events because I couldn't count on myself. I am always in pain, tire easily, forget people's names and important events, have experienced vertigo, feel nauseous frequently, and battle general malaise, but struggle to share these changes with others. So, I put on the mask and tried to pretend I was fine, but there were cracks in my façade. I was wearing down, so I stayed home more and more. I withdrew from friends and family and am still working my way back to healthy relationships. I had always been athletic, strong, resilient, so the shame I felt from such a drastic change in functioning piled on top of constant pain left me unmoored. I felt like a stranger in a strange land, untethered and afraid ... of both my present and my future. But, I am trying to find a way back to myself, my family and friends, and to God.

Fibromyalgia is a confusing, all-consuming, and unsettling chronic pain condition that has no cure. Perhaps you have heard of it but don't have any idea what it means, what the symptoms are, or what causes the condition.

According to the Cleveland Clinic, "Fibromyalgia is a long-term (chronic) health condition that causes pain and tenderness throughout your body. It causes musculoskeletal pain and fatigue ... Experts don't know what causes fibromyalgia, but studies have found that certain health conditions, stress and other changes in your life might trigger it. You might be more likely to develop fibromyalgia if one of your biological parents has it."[5]

No one in my family has fibromyalgia, but several family members have suffered with conditions that are painful, chronic, and sometimes both, like lupus and polymyalgia rheumatica. My personal experience is that those of us with these conditions are sensitive souls who live life deeply, feel emotions strongly, and experience them in every part of our being. Because we feel deeply, we often take on the pain of others and it begins to live inside of us along with our own pain, joining forces and growing larger, more intense. If we are not careful, this pain can stress our systems and we end up carrying more than our minds or bodies were designed for. It is widely accepted that we carry stress not only in our minds but in our bodies as well. Memories live in our cells, and if we have unresolved pain, trauma, and lingering complex issues, they can manifest in all kinds of health conditions. Our bodies speak. We would be wise to listen.

> Matthew 11:28-30, "Come to me, all you who are weary and burdened and I will give you rest. Take my yoke upon you and learn from me, for I am gentle and humble in heart, and you will find rest for your souls. For my yoke is easy and my burden is light."

Learning about this condition has been a journey for me. It is hallmarked by a litany of seemingly unconnected symptoms

---

[5] (Fibromyalgia: Symptoms, Diagnosis & Treatment (clevelandclinic.org))

that are puzzling at best to those of us who suffer with them, so I can imagine how confusing it is for those who don't. Symptoms can affect every part of our bodies including widespread pain, fatigue, brain fog/cognitive difficulties, digestive problems, headaches, memory problems, anxiety, depression, sleep issues and more because it is believed to be a central nervous system condition that amplifies pain signals. When your body is in a constant state of fight-or-flight, this hyperstate leaves you strung out and exhausted. As I have learned, unmanaged pain simply begets more pain. It wears you down and hope seems to drift ever farther out of reach. It's a terrible spiral. However, I always try to look for the good, to reach for the light by searching every situation for an opportunity to learn, grow, and draw closer to the Lord, asking, *What Lord, are you trying to teach me?* rather than, *Why Lord, is this happening to me?* I believe God is using this season to teach me to listen to my body, revealing unseen and unsaid things. These things whisper truths we need to know but often go unnoticed—unattended to—like unforgiveness, shame, anxiety, fear, etc. God wants to heal these aspects of our human condition.

> "Therefore we do not lose heart. Though outwardly we are wasting away, yet inwardly we are being renewed day by day. For our light and momentary troubles are achieving for us an eternal glory that far outweighs them all. So we fix our eyes not on what is seen, but on what is unseen, since what is seen is temporary, but what is unseen is eternal."
> (2 Corinthians 4:14-18)

Some people call Fibromyalgia a "garbage" diagnosis. Some say it isn't real. Some don't know anyone who has it, so they have no first-hand experience. I hope my story gives you a peek into the life of someone with this condition and leaves you with more compassion and understanding. This diagnosis causes me pain everywhere all the time; I am never free of it, not even when I sleep. I struggle to get up in the morning with pain so deep, so wide, it takes everything I have to get myself out of bed and face the day. Stiffness and pain are often worse in the morning, and I wonder each day if I can do it all again ... and just when I think I can't, God reminds me I am His, that He has made me for a purpose. So, before getting out of bed, I pray. I thank God for the day and ask Him to help me discover my purpose, accomplish His will, and ease my pain. The verse that so often comes to me in those early morning moments is when Jesus spoke to his disciples saying, "With man this is impossible, but with God all things are possible." (Matthew 19:26) Together, with God, we can do what we could not do alone, whether that is to endure, to celebrate, to weather storms, or experience victory. We don't know His plans for us, but we can trust Him to give us the strength we need to do His will.

Healing is a priority for me now, and it comes in many ways. It might not look the way I want it to, but I am working on acceptance and praising Him regardless. I have a prescription filled in case I decide to go that route. There is no judgment here—no *wrong* or *right*—only what works and what doesn't. I am experimenting with lifestyle changes and various alternative therapies. I am interested in reiki and acupuncture, and I hope to see an integrative or functional doctor in the future. Nutrition is important to combat digestive issues, and I have learned a lot from online fibro conferences chock full of cutting-edge research and practices. Rhythms, rituals, and habits like writing and journaling, walking on my local nature trail, yoga, and stretching (for 2 minutes – it makes a big difference!) help ease the pain, loosen up my body, and calm my mind. I have found several online groups where fibro sufferers share information and support, I read books (see the resource section) about fibromyalgia, pain, somatic practices, and I have begun to share my story.

Fibromyalgia has both caused me to withdraw *and* forced me to reach out for help. When times are tough and the pain and dysfunction in my body threaten to overtake me, I remember that God's Word is never out of reach; it is always available. There is no barrier between me and God, least I put it there. All I need to do is reach for Him, to pray, to read scripture, to call a trusted friend. I have learned to recognize the Lord's voice. He *speaks* to me through scripture, prayer, music, books, and the loving people in my life, providing comfort and direction when I seek Him. He is ever present and the ability to hear has more to do with the level of my own awareness than his availability. God is everywhere, all at once, and all knowing.

My faith and family are the reasons I am still here fighting today. The Lord is my shelter, my rock, my deliverer. I don't know what God has planned for me, but I am going to walk with Him daily, seek Him first, and take the small consistent steps of faith He calls me to take. I sometimes wonder if God allowed me to experience this condition because He wants me to be still, to draw nearer and focus on Him, listening for the messages he designed specifically for me, and the ones He wants me to share with others. I am not saying God caused my fibromyalgia, but He allowed it, perhaps as a pruning process. He reminds me at every turn that He is in control; He is provider, protector, healer, counselor. He is my All in All, the Alpha and Omega. If I believe that, I must trust Him. There is no other way. *Jesus Christ is the way, the truth, and the life* ... and that gives me the hope of being found again.

****

About the Author:

Allison Hrip is an author, book editor, and storyteller. Using her years of writing and editing experience combined with her keen intuition, she helps budding writers and authors elevate their words and bring their stories to life. She writes about living a creative life, spirituality, grief, nature, and the connection between mind, body, and spirit. Allison is a wife and mom to three adult children and a rescue dog.

Connect with Allison:
allisonhrip@gmail.com
Facebook: https://www.facebook.com/allison.hrip.9/
Instagram: www.instagram.com/allisonhrip
LinkedIn: www.linkedin.com/in/allisonhrip

Resources:
https://www.myfibroteam.com/ (online support group)
Mayo Clinic Guide to Fibromyalgia by Andy Abril, M.D. and Barbara K. Bruce, PH.D., L.P. (book)
National Fibromyalgia Association, FM and chronic pain (fmaware.org)
Education, Research, & Advocacy | National Fibromyalgia Nonprofit (supportfibromyalgia.org)

My Pain Journey from a Physical, Mental, and Spiritual Perspective

By Rick Miller

My Pain Journey from a Physical, Mental, and Spiritual Perspective. I ask myself, are the three joined, related, or cause and effect? The current facts/status. I have been dealing with an autoimmune disease for quite a few years. I was always able to hide the chronic pain and deal with it.

It was not until December 2020, when I contracted the Covid 19 virus, that the roller coaster truly began in full effect. I have always (right or wrong) placed a lot of my own self-worth in my work and ability to take care of my family.

This allowed me to support my family/daughters comfortably. I do not mean that we were wealthy, but my girls had everything they needed and a little of what they wanted. I was a self-reliant man. I mean, I took care of our automobiles, home repairs and renovations myself. In fact, several of my hobbies included automotive repairs and carpentry. I am no longer able to complete even the simplest of physical or day-to- day tasks.

My wife assists me with the simple tasks such as dressing, putting on the boot that assists me in walking and many others. I can cautiously navigate noticeably short distances with a cane. I require a power wheelchair to go further distances.

I have been diagnosed with Post-Covid, Degenerative Disc Disease of the spine, a pituitary tumor at the base of my brain, Cushing's Disease, Fibromyalgia, an autoimmune disease, along with an additional host of others. This is just to list a few of the physical issues and impacts.

The chronic pain has resulted in significant downtime and insomnia. This is when the mental impacts began their assault. As I stated previously, I placed my self-worth in my ability to take care of things myself. I can no longer take care of our vehicles, house repairs or even carrying in groceries. I do not see the value that I bring to my family. In fact, I began thinking of the burden that I have become to my family. I would be authoring an entire novel If I were to list in detail all the mental aspects, thoughts, and battles in just the past three years. I will just leave it at how these thoughts lead to depression and anxiety.

However, it is this slowdown that has given me a new reflective process. It is within this reflection that God is revealing to me the proper perspective of love, self-worth, and value. It is not the things that I can do for my family that are the most important. As it states in 1 Corinthians 13:13 "..the greatest of these is love". It is this quiet and stillness that has forced me to listen and witness God's work in my life. I heard a Christian comedian on a social media video speaking about his journey to Christ from being an atheist. The one phrase that struck me the most was "the hound of heaven." It is where God pursues us until we stop and listen. This may also include pain to have us listen not because God wants to hurt us but because that is what it may take for us to listen. This just brings home the revelation for me with my current situation.

In summary, I must be honest and transparent here. I have always been more of a class half empty kind of guy. God sent me one of the greatest blessings in my life, my wife. She is the exact opposite. It is her encouragement, along with the love of my three daughters, that has kept me from focusing on the negative. It repeatedly reminds me when the pain is bad (and I am very cranky) that God will take care of us. This directly addresses my great worry of not being able to take care of my girls. If God is for us, who can be against us (Romans 8:31). "The LORD himself goes before you and will be with you; he will never leave you nor forsake you. Do not be afraid; do not be discouraged," (Deuteronomy 31:8).

****

My Season of Pain

By Beeda L. Speis

In January 2022, I attended a missions conference that had attendees from all over the world. A few days after returning home, I felt awful. Nothing stood out as wrong, but I knew it wasn't the average flu. I took a Covid test, which came back negative. After a week, the cold and flu symptoms disappeared, only to be replaced with something more concerning. I had extreme pain all over my body. It couldn't be defined as joint or muscle pain; it was just pain. Sometimes, it felt like I was being stabbed with a knife, and other times, like someone was sticking me with hundreds of needles. No over-the-counter medicine could touch it.

However, the thing that interrupted my life the most was fatigue. I couldn't do anything but lay around or watch T.V. It was as if all energy had been taken from me. I missed about six weeks of work.

I went to Urgent Care, but they couldn't find anything wrong with me. I went to my family doctor, but he just said to wait a few weeks and see if it goes away. Several weeks later, he was surprised to see me again with no change to my symptoms. I presented him with an article I read about Long Covid and how they found it in people who had a mild case of Covid that wasn't necessarily confirmed by a test. He disagreed. Since I didn't have a positive test, he couldn't and wouldn't label it Long Covid. After talking a while longer, he said it could be Chronic Fatigue Syndrome, which is an autonomic disorder, also known as Dysautonomia.

I went to Cleveland Clinic for several tests, which ruled out small fiber neuropathy; therefore, it *must* be Fibromyalgia (as if those were the only two options). I've since been told that Fibromyalgia is more of a catch-all diagnosis for chronic pain. My family doctor isn't ready to accept that answer. He continues to try different medications to help with my symptoms. I'm very blessed that he is trying so hard to help me, no matter what label is put on the cause of my pain and fatigue.

With that information, I could do my own research and joined a few Facebook Groups, which were very helpful. They shared similar stories to what I'd already been through. They told me I was *not* crazy, and it was *not* in my head. What a blessing to have talked to them before I saw my first specialist, a cardiologist who took care of me while I was on a very aggressive chemotherapy regimen years before. I was so surprised at him. He looked at my chart, saw that I was on antidepressants and anti-anxiety medicine, and then, without asking me any other questions except how many hours I worked, concluded that I was just stressed and needed to exercise. There was a time when I would have believed him, but no more.

The way the medical field is run now, they throw us all into the same box. If we're overweight or are on antidepressants or whatever, they'll use it as an excuse not to treat our pain. They'll try to make us believe our pain is the result of something that we caused, and therefore, we can fix it ourselves without pain medicine.

Fortunately, as Christians, we can get through these challenging situations because we have a Heavenly Father who loves us. He may not take our pain away, but He'll help us through the storm.

Before I got sick, I was very active in my church and with a community of Christian writers. I had some sort of meeting or project to work on nearly every evening after work.

After I got sick, I couldn't do any of it. I didn't know what I was supposed to do for the Kingdom when I felt as bad as I did. I started praying about it. God showed me the way. I could write and connect with people one on one. I have a Facebook prayer group, and I found a way, thanks to God, to finally start publishing instead of just talking about it all of the time. It gave me renewed confidence in prayer and in God's sovereignty over all things.

Even now, just over two years into this mystery illness, I'm still thrown for a loop whenever I have a flare-up. The months in between are pretty "normal," and I feel so blessed to have those breaks from the pain and fatigue, but when it comes back, I ask God what He wants me to do, knowing that He has a plan to use me even when it seems impossible. That plan actually helps distract me from the pain, and it brings my focus back to Him, and to those He sends my way.

As James wrote, "My brethren, count it all joy when you fall into various trials, knowing that the testing of your faith produces patience." James 1:2-3 NKJV

****

About the Author:

Beeda L. Speis is a Christian Author who writes about finding the peace and hope we have in Jesus. Her daily posts can be found in her Facebook Group, "Pray in the Stillness" where she uses real-life experiences to show the omnipresence of our loving, caring, Heavenly Father. Her debut devotional, Dear God: I'm in Pain, has an international readership. It's available in both English, Spanish, and as an audiobook, and has a companion pain tracker, and journal available. Visit linktr.ee/beedaspeis for more information and to follow her on social media.

One more thing…

Please consider visiting the authors' books, websites, and social media profiles shared in this book. It really helps indie authors stand out.

Also, please leave a review of this book by visiting
https://www.amazon.com/dp/B0DT7SY49T

Hope When it Hurts: Where Chronic Pain and Faith Collide was originally published as *Letters from the Fold: Seeing God in a Season of Pain.* Some reviews from the First Edition:

Letters from the Fold is a beautifully encouraging book for those who face chronic pain. Each letter shares heart-wrenching stories of suffering interlaced with God's grace, love, and mercy. The faith shared by each person in their journey is encouraging and uplifting.
  I highly recommend this book to anyone suffering through their own season of suffering and truly to anyone who needs to borrow from the faith of those who have walked before them.
  Thank you to each person who contributed to this book. So many will be blessed through your testimonies.

★★★★★

Whether you have chronic pain or not this book will inspire you.

★★★★★

Letters from the Fold dives into the spiritual and emotional dimensions of enduring chronic pain through a series of personal narratives. Each letter offers a unique glimpse into the struggles and triumphs of individuals facing life's harsh realities, supported by their deeply rooted faith. This book is a resource for anyone seeking to understand the intersection of suffering and spirituality. It also benefits spiritual leaders and caregivers looking to deepen their empathy and enhance their supportive capacities. Having lived on both sides of this, I found the stories are revealing and inspiring, highlighting the profound strength of faith and community. Cannot recommend it highly enough.

[The contributors] talk about how God shows Himself through their lives now. Inspiring.

Letters from the Fold's testimonial collections were immense and profoundly moving. They offered hope and encouragement to anyone suffering chronic pain or illness. Each story is raw and authentic, revealing how individuals have learned to use their faith to navigate times of suffering when medical solutions are scarce. The letters comfort those in pain and are insightful for pastors, counselors, family, and anyone looking to understand how God can bring peace and strength through hardship. This book reminded me that I am not alone and beautifully highlights God's presence in our most difficult moments. Comfort and inspiration are the trademarks of this book.

Made in the USA
Columbia, SC
21 June 2025

59704799R00048